DE '97

The CHRISTMAS FAKE BOOK

More than 150 songs

Featuring Your All Time Favorite Popular And Traditional
Christmas Carols And Songs

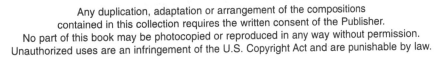
Cover Design/Calligraphy: Raine W. Clotfelter
Production Coordinator: Tom Roed

CONTENTS

ALL HAIL TO THEE

TRADITIONAL

ALL THROUGH THE NIGHT

TRADITIONAL

ANGELS FROM HEAVEN

TRADITIONAL HUNGARIAN
Translated by Bernard Gasso

1. An - gels from Heav - en spoke to the shep - herds, "Tid - ings we
2. An - gels from Heav - en spoke to the shep - herds, "You will see

bring to thee, tid - ings from Beth - le - hem, from a man - ger.
One who'll be Lord of the fu - ture, King and Re - deem - er,

On this morn, Christ was born."
Son of God, Son of God!"

ANGELS FROM THE REALMS OF GLORY

Words by JAMES MONTGOMERY
Music by HENRY SMART

1. An - gels from the realms of glo - ry, wing your flight o'er
2. Shep - herds in the fields a - bid - ing, watch - ing o'er your
3. Sag - es, leave your con - tem - pla - tions; bright - er vi - sions
4. Saints be - fore the al - tar bend - ing, watch - ing long in

all the earth. Ye who sang cre - a - tion's sto - ry,
flocks by night. God with man is now re - sid - ing,
beam a - far. Seek the great de - sire of na - tions;
hope and fear. Sud - den - ly the Lord de - scend - ing

now pro - claim Mes - si - ah's birth.
yon - der shines the ___ in - fant light.
ye have seen His ___ na - tal star.
in His tem - ple ___ shall ap - pear.

Come and wor - ship,

come and wor - ship; wor - ship Christ the new - born King. new - born King.

ANGELS WE HAVE HEARD ON HIGH

Copyright © 1990 by BEAM ME UP MUSIC, c/o CPP/BELWIN, INC.
All Rights Reserved

TRADITIONAL

AS LATELY WE WATCHED

Copyright © 1990 by BEAM ME UP MUSIC, c/o CPP/BELWIN, INC.
All Rights Reserved

TRADITIONAL

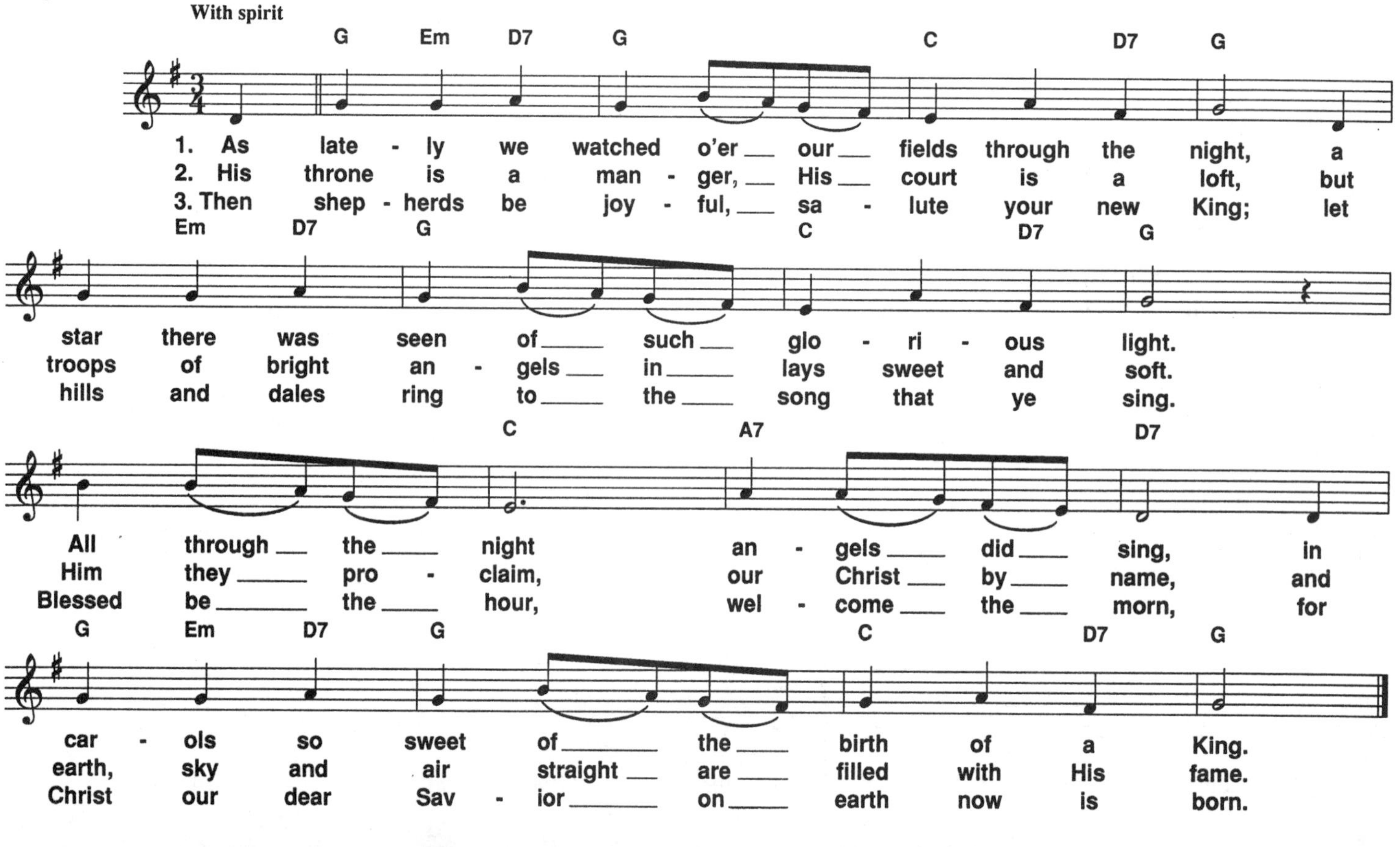

AS WITH GLADNESS MEN OF OLD

Words by WILLIAM C. DIX
Music by CONRAD KOCHER

1. As with gladness men of old did the guiding
2. As with joyful steps they sped to that lowly
3. As they offered gifts most rare at that manger
4. Holy Jesus every day keep us in the

star behold. As with joy they hailed its light
manger bed. There to bend the knee before
rude and bare, so may we with holy joy,
narrow way. And when earthly things are past,

leading onward, beaming bright. So most gracious
Him who heav'n and earth adore. So may we with
pure and free from sin's alloy. All our costliest
bring our ransomed souls at last where they need no

1.2.3.
God, may we evermore be led by Thee.
willing feet ever seek Thy mercy seat.
treasures bring Christ to Thee, our heav'nly king.
star to guide, where no clouds Thy

4.
glory hide.

AULD LANG SYNE

Words by ROBERT BURNS
Music TRADITIONAL

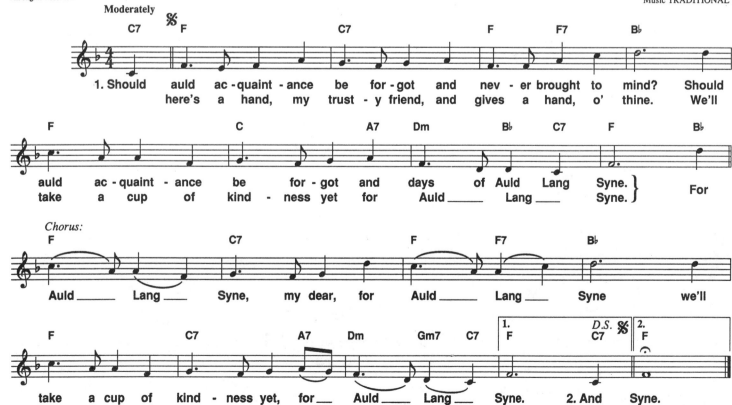

1. Should auld acquaintance be forgot and never brought to mind? Should
here's a hand, my trusty friend, and gives a hand, o' thine. We'll

auld acquaintance be forgot and days of Auld Lang Syne. For
take a cup of kindness yet for Auld Lang Syne. For

Chorus:

Auld Lang Syne, my dear, for Auld Lang Syne we'll

1.
take a cup of kindness yet, for Auld Lang Syne.
2. And Syne.

F3021FBX

AVE MARIA
(Schubert)

Text by REV. BURTON AMES
Music by FRANZ SCHUBERT

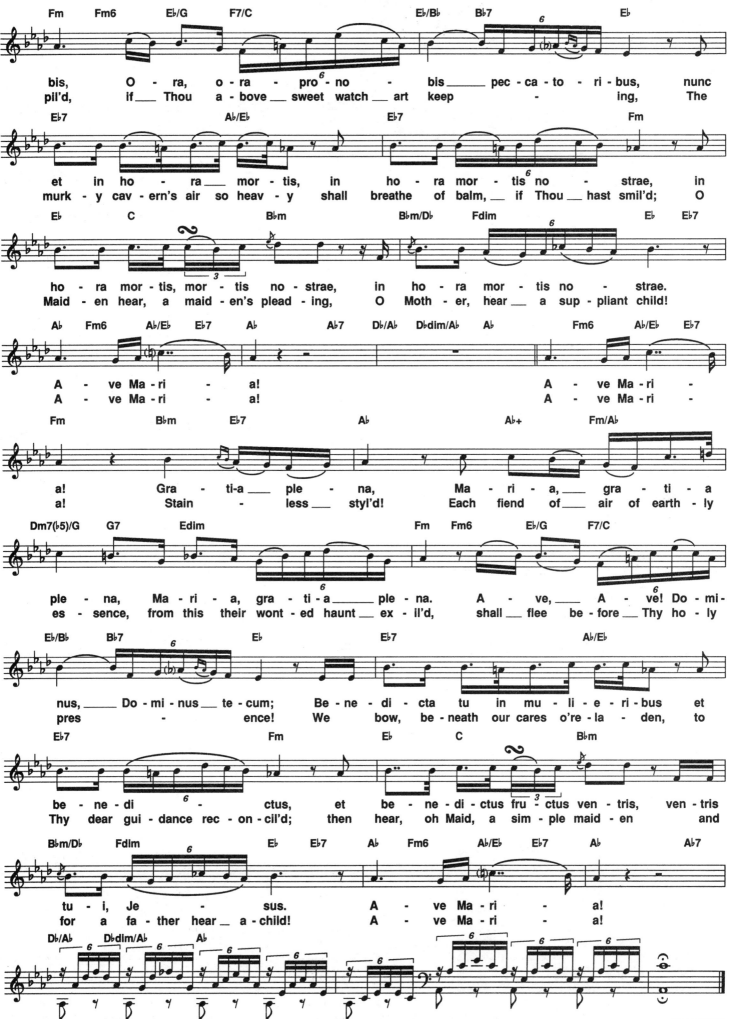

11

F3021FBX

AVE MARIA
(Bach - Gounod)

From The First Prelude of
JOHANN SEBASTIAN BACH
Adapted by CHARLES GOUNOD

AWAY IN A MANGER

LUTHER/SPILLMAN

Sweetly

A - way in A__ Man - ger, no crib for His bed, The lit - tle Lord Je - sus lay down His sweet head; The stars in the __ heav - ens looked down where He lay, The lit - tle Lord Je - sus, a - sleep in the hay. The __ cat - tle are low - ing, the poor ba - by wakes, But __ lit - tle Lord Je - sus no cry - ing __ He __ makes; I love Thee, Lord __ Je - sus, look down from the sky, And stay by my cra - dle to watch lul - la - by.

AWAY IN A MANGER

By J.R. MURRAY

Tender lullaby

1. A - way in a man - ger, no crib for a bed, the
(2.) cat - tle are low - ing, the Ba - by a - wakes, But
(3.) near me, Lord Je - sus; I ask Thee to stay close

lit - tle Lord Je - sus laid down His sweet head. The
lit - tle Lord Je - sus, no cry - ing He makes. I
by me for - ev - er and love me I pray. Bless

stars in the sky ____ looked down where He lay. The
love Thee, Lord Je - sus; look down from the sky and
all the dear chil - dren in Thy ten - der care, and

lit - tle Lord Je - sus, a - sleep on the hay. 2. The
stay by my cra - dle till morn - ing is nigh. 3. Be
take us to heav - en to live with Thee there.

A-CAROLING WE GO

Words and Music by
JOHNNY MARKS

Moderately bright

C — Am — Dm — G7sus — G7

1. A car - ol - ing, a car - ol - ing, a car - ol - ing we go,
bring you sea - son's greet - ings and we wish the best to you,
you may have your hol - ly and per - haps some mis - tle - toe,
car - ol - ing, a car - ol - ing, a car - ol - ing we go,

Am — Em — Am7 — D9 — G7

Hearts filled with mu - sic and cheeks a - glow. _____ From
And may our wish last the whole year through. _____ Come
May - be a fir tree and may - be snow. _____ But
Hearts filled with mu - sic and cheeks a - glow. _____ From

C — Am — Dm — G7sus — G7

house to house we bring the mes - sage of the King a - gain,
join us if you will as we are sing - ing once a - gain,
would - n't it be won - der - ful if we could have a - gain,
house to house we bring the mes - sage of the King a - gain,

Am — Em — Am — F — Bm7(♭5) — E — Am — Em — Am

Peace On ____ Earth, Good Will To Men, Peace On ____ Earth, Good

1.2.3.
F — G7 — C — F — G7 — C
4.
F — G7 — C

Will To Men.

Will To Men. ____

2. We
3. Now
4. A

A BABE IS BORN IN BETHLEHEM

LUDWIG LINDEMAN

Moderately

C — F — C — G7 — C — Am

1. A Babe is born in Beth - le - hem, in
2. He doth with - in a man - ger lie; a
3. The wise men came, led by the star; led
4. On this most bless - ed Ju - bi - lee; blest

G7 — C — G — Bm — Em — Am7 — D7 — G

Beth - le - hem; There - fore re - joice Je - ru - sa - lem. Al -
man - ger lie; Whose throne is set a - bove the sky. Al -
by the star; Gold, myrrh and in - cense, brought from far. Al -
Ju - bi - lee; All glo - ry be, O God, to Thee. Al -

G7 — C — G7 — C — G7 — C

le - lu - jah, Al - le - lu - jah.
le - lu - jah, Al - le - lu - jah.
le - lu - jah, Al - le - lu - jah.
le - lu - jah, Al - le - lu - jah.

BEHOLD THAT STAR

By THOMAS W. TALLEY

BIRTHDAY OF A KING

By WILLIAM HOWARD NEIDLINGER

F3021FBX

THE BOAR'S HEAD CAROL

TRADITIONAL

BREAK FORTH, O BEAUTEOUS HEAVENLY LIGHT

TRADITIONAL

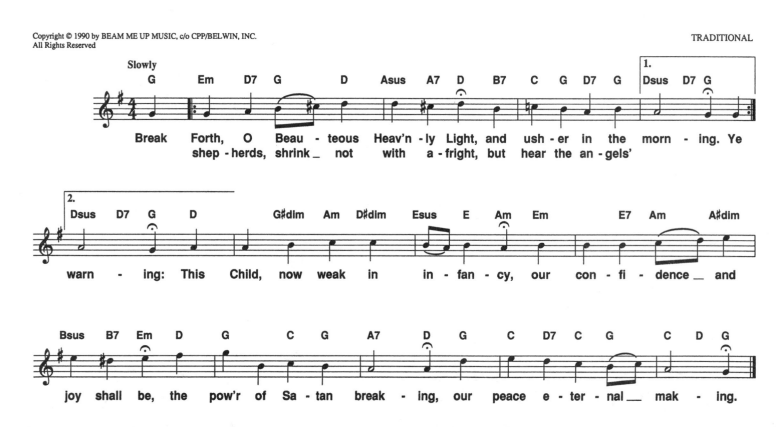

BRING A TORCH, JEANNETTE, ISABELLA

TRADITIONAL

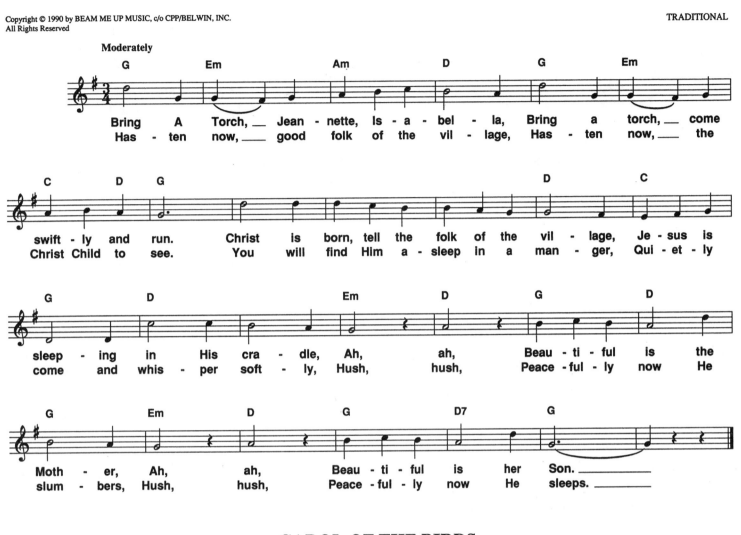

Bring A Torch, __ Jean - nette, Is - a - bel - la, Bring a torch, __ come
Has - ten now, __ good folk of the vil - lage, Has - ten now, __ the

swift - ly and run. Christ is born, tell the folk of the vil - lage, Je - sus is
Christ Child to see. You will find Him a - sleep in a man - ger, Qui - et - ly

sleep - ing in His cra - dle, Ah, ah, Beau - ti - ful is the
come and whis - per soft - ly, Hush, hush, Peace - ful - ly now He

Moth - er, Ah, ah, Beau - ti - ful is her Son. ___
slum - bers, Hush, hush, Peace - ful - ly now He sleeps. ___

CAROL OF THE BIRDS

TRADITIONAL

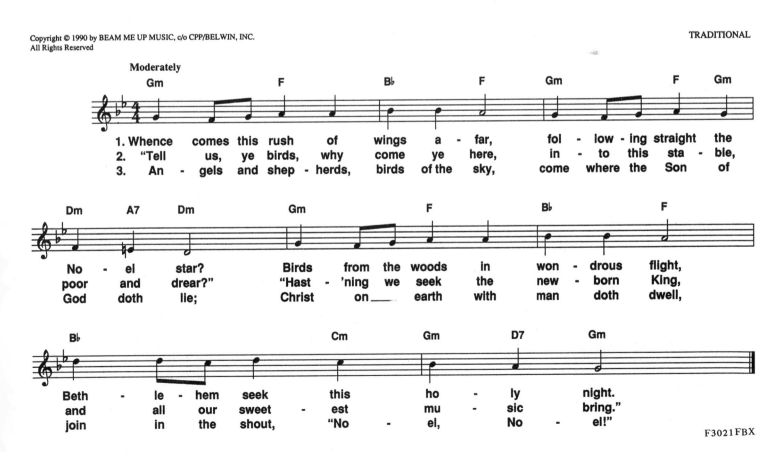

1. Whence comes this rush of wings a - far, fol - low - ing straight the
2. "Tell us, ye birds, why come ye here, in - to this sta - ble,
3. An - gels and shep - herds, birds of the sky, come where the Son of

No - el star? Birds from the woods in won - drous flight,
poor and drear?" "Hast - 'ning we seek the new - born King,
God doth lie; Christ on __ earth with man doth dwell,

Beth - le - hem seek this ho - ly night.
and all our sweet - est mu - sic bring."
join in the shout, "No - el, No - el!"

F3021FBX

THE CHERRY TREE CAROL

TRADITIONAL

1. As Jo - seph was a - walk - ing, he heard an an - gel sing, "This night shall be the birth - time of Christ the heav'n - ly King. He nei - ther shall be born in hous - en nor in hall, nor in the place of par - a - dise, but in an ox - 's stall.

2. He nei - ther shall be clothed In pur - ple nor in pall, but in the fair white lin - en that us - en ba - bies all. He nei - ther shall be rocked in sil - ver nor in gold, but in a wood - en man - ger, that rest - eth on the mould.

A CHILD IS BORN IN BETHLEHEM

TRADITIONAL

1. A Child is born in Beth - le - hem, in Beth - le - hem, and glad - ness fills Je - ru - sa - lem, Al - le - lu - ja, al - le - lu - ja!

2. Un - to a maid - en so for - lorn, oh so for - lorn, a Son, the Son of God was born, Al - le - lu - ja, al - le - lu - ja!

3. A low - ly man - ger shel - tered Him, This Ho - ly Boy. God's an - gels sang a - bove with joy, Al - le - lu - ja, al - le - lu - ja!

4. We now give thanks e - ter - na - ly, E - ter - nal - ly. To God, the Ho - ly Trin - i - ty, Al - le - lu - ja, al - le - lu - ja!

CHILDREN, GO WHERE I SEND THEE

TRADITIONAL

Freely

Chil - dren, go where I send thee. How shall I send __ thee?

Moderately Bright

1. I'm gon - na send thee one by one. One's for the lit - tle it - ty Ba - by,

Born, born __ Lord, born in Beth - le - hem. Chil - dren,

go where I send thee. How shall I send __ thee?

Repeat as necessary

Moderately bright *(Verse)*

2. I'm gon - na send thee two by two, ___ 'cause two was a Paul and
3. I'm gon - na send thee three by three, ___ 'cause three was the He - brew
4. I'm gon - na send thee four by four, ___ 'cause four was the poor came
5. I'm gon - na send thee five by five, ___ 'cause five was the gos - pel

Si - las, and one was the lit - tle it - ty Ba - by.
chil - dren, and (to 2.)
knock - in' on the door, and (to 3.)
preach - ers, and (to 4.)

For additional verses — F *Freely* | *Last time* — F

Born, born __ Lord, born in Beth - le - hem. Chil - dren hem.

Continue similarly

6. Six for the six that couldn't be fixed,
7. Seven for the seven that went up to heaven,
8. Eight for the eight that stood at the gate,
9. Nine for the nine that got left behind,
10. Ten for the Ten Commandments,

F3021FBX

CHRIST WAS BORN ON CHRISTMAS DAY

TRADITIONAL

Moderately bright

(Verse 1) Christ Was Born On Christ - mas Day, Wreath the hol - ly, twine the bay; *Christ - us na - tus ho - di - e;* The Babe, the Son, the Ho - ly One of Ma - ry.

2. He is born to set us free,
He is born our Lord to be,
Ex Maria Virgine;
The God, The Lord, by all adored forever.

3. Let the bright red berries glow,
Everywhere in goodly show;
Christus natus hodie;
The Babe, the Son, the Holy One of Mary.

4. Christian men rejoice and sing,
'Tis the birthday of a King,
Ex Maria Virgine;
The God, the Lord, by all adored forever.

CHRISTIANS, AWAKE! SALUTE THE HAPPY MORN

TRADITIONAL

Chris - tians, A - wake! Sa - lute The Hap - py Morn, Where - on the Sav - iour of the
Then to the watch - ful shep - herds it was told, Who heard th'an - gel - ic her - ald's

world was born; Rise to a - dore the mys - ter - y of love,
voice, "Be - hold, I bring good ti - dings of a Sav - iour's birth

Which hosts of an - gels chant - ed from a - bove; With them the joy - ful
To you and all the na - tions up - on earth; This day hath God ful -

ti - dings first be - gun Of God in - car - nate and the Vir - gin's Son.
filled His prom - ised word; This day is born a Sav - iour, Christ the Lord."

3. He spake; and straightway the celestial choir
In hymns of joy, unknown before, conspire;
The praises of redeeming love they sang,
And heaven's whole orb with alleluias rang;
God's highest glory was their anthem still,
Peace upon the earth, and unto men good will.

4. Then may we hope, th' angelic hosts among.
To sing, redeemed, a glad triumphal song;
He that was born upon this joyful day
Around us all His glory shall display;
Saved by His love, incessant we shall sing
Eternal praise to heaven's Almighty King.

CHRISTMAS

By JACKIE DE SHANNON, JIMMY HOLIDAY
and RANDY MEYERS

Moderately

Chorus:

This is the sea-son for giv-ing, ___ Can't you feel it in the air? There is a rea-son for liv-ing ___ And a rea-son to care.

Fine *Verse:*

1. I love to watch the lit-tle chil-dren bless their hearts, be-cause it's such a spe-cial day for them.
2. I see the fire-light shin-ing, how much it means to be to-geth-er at this time of year.

Dolls and trains are all a-part, Rein-deer and fall-ing snow, The hang-ing mis-tle-toe

Ev-'ry-thing's in place it seems, Pres-ents un-der the tree, There's one from you to me

songs of Beth-le-hem. }
Lis-ten can't you hear.

Ah ___ Christ-mas

Ah ___ Christ-mas ___ Christ-mas.

F3021FBX

CHRISTMAS AT OUR HOUSE

Words and Music by
DON PFRIMMER and
ARCHIE JORDAN

CHRISTMAS EVE IN MY HOME TOWN

Words and Music by
STAN ZABKA and
DON UPTON

CHRISTMAS LULLABY

Lyric by PEGGY LEE
Music by CY COLEMAN

CHRISTMAS TIME IS HERE

(From "A Charlie Brown Christmas")

By LEE MENDELSON
and VINCE GUARALDI

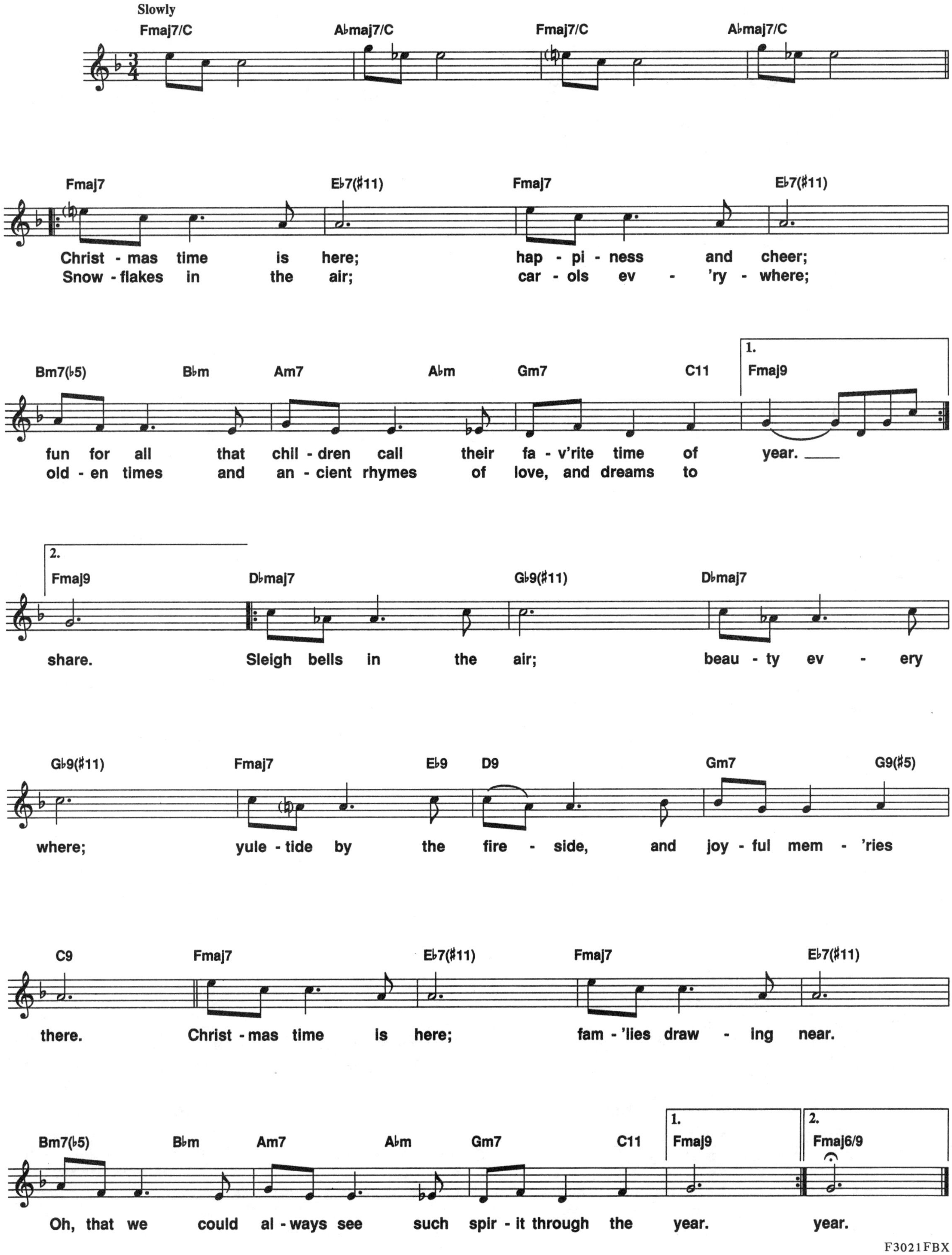

Slowly
Fmaj7/C Abmaj7/C Fmaj7/C Abmaj7/C
Fmaj7 Eb7(#11) Fmaj7 Eb7(#11)
Christ - mas time is here; hap - pi - ness and cheer;
Snow - flakes in the air; car - ols ev - 'ry - where;
Bm7(b5) Bbm Am7 Abm Gm7 C11 1. Fmaj9
fun for all that chil - dren call their fa - v'rite time of year.
old - en times and an - cient rhymes of love, and dreams to
2. Fmaj9 Dbmaj7 Gb9(#11) Dbmaj7
share. Sleigh bells in the air; beau - ty ev - ery
Gb9(#11) Fmaj7 Eb9 D9 Gm7 G9(#5)
where; yule - tide by the fire - side, and joy - ful mem - 'ries
C9 Fmaj7 Eb7(#11) Fmaj7 Eb7(#11)
there. Christ - mas time is here; fam - 'lies draw - ing near.
Bm7(b5) Bbm Am7 Abm Gm7 C11 1. Fmaj9 2. Fmaj6/9
Oh, that we could al - ways see such spir - it through the year. year.

A CHRISTMAS TO REMEMBER

Words and Music by
DOLLY PARTON

4. You made this a Christmas to remember.
   Springtime feelin's in the middle of December.
   Though the fire is hot,
   We'll just have to let it simmer.
   Oh! What a Christmas to remember!

5. You made this a Christmas to remember
   Springtime feelin's in the middle of December.
   Though it's cold outside,
   We'll just stroke the burning embers.
   Oh! What a Christmas to remember!

6. You made this a Christmas to remember,
   As the icicles hang from the
   Roofs and on the windows.
   Though the fire is hot,
   We'll just have to let it simmer.
   Oh! What a Christmas to remember.

COME, THOU LONG-EXPECTED JESUS

TRADITIONAL

Come, Thou Long - Ex - pect - ed Je - sus, Born to set Thy
Born Thy peo - ple to de - liv - er, Born a child and

peo - ple free; From our fears and sins re - lease us;
yet a King. Born to reign in us for - ev - er,

Let us find our rest in Thee. Is - rael's strength and con - so -
Now Thy gra - cious king - dom bring. By Thine own e - ter - nal

la - tion, Hope of all the earth Thou art; Dear de -
Spir - it Rule in all our hearts a - lone; By Thine

sire of ev - ery na - tion, Joy of ev - ery long - ing heart.
all - suf - fi - cient mer - it, Raise us too Thy glo - rious throne.

THE COVENTRY CAROL
(Lullay, Thou Little Tiny Child)

TRADITIONAL

Gently, like a lullaby

1. Lul - lay, Thou lit - tle ti - ny Child, bye - bye, lul -
2. O sis - ters, too, how may we do for to pre -
3. Her - od the King in his rag - ing charg - ed he
4. Then woe is me, poor Child for Thee, and ev - er

loo, lul - lay. Lul - lay, Thou lit - tle ti - ny
serve this day? This poor Young - ling for whom we
hath this day his men of might in his own
morn and day. For Thy part - ing nor say, nor

Child, bye - bye, lul - loo, lul - lay.
sing, bye - bye, lul - loo, lul - lay.
sight, all chil - dren young to slay.
sing, bye - bye, lul - loo, lul- lay.

DECK THE HALL

OLD WELSH AIR

1. Deck the hall with boughs of hol - ly.
2. See the blaz - ing yule be - fore us.
3. Fast a - way the old year pass - es.
} Fa la la la la la la la la.

'Tis the sea - son to be jol - ly.
Strike the harp and join the cho - rus.
Hail the new, ye lads and lass - es.
} Fa la la la la la la la la.

Don we now our gay ap - par - el.
Fol - low me in mer - ry mea - sure,
Sing we joy - ous all to - geth - er,
} Fa la la la la la la la la.

Troll the an - cient yule - tide car - ol.
while I tell of yule - tide trea - sure.
heed - less of the wind and weath - er.
} Fa la la la la la la la la. la la la.

EVERYONE'S A CHILD AT CHRISTMAS

Words and Music by
JOHNNY MARKS

Ev - 'ry-one's A Child At Christ - mas ____ And looks for pres - ents un - der the Christ - mas

tree. ____ Ev - 'ry-one's A Child At Christ - mas ____ And loves the hap - py hol - i - day jol - li -

ty. ____ You must al - ways be - lieve, that on each Christ - mas Eve, Old San - ta

Claus will be com - ing be - cause you're good, Did ev - 'ry - thing you should. Ev - 'ry-one's A Child At

Christ - mas, ____ For Christ - mas is for chil - dren like you and me. ____ me. ____

F3021FBX

THE FIRST NOEL

TRADITIONAL

Moderately slow

1. The _____ first _____ No - el, the _____
2. (They _____) look - ed _____ up and _____
3. (This _____) star _____ drew _____ nigh to _____

an - gel did say, was to cer - tain poor
saw _____ a star, shin - ing in _____ the
the _____ north - west; o - ver Beth - le -

shep - herds in fields as they lay; in _____
East _____ be - yond _____ them far; and _____
hem _____ it took _____ its rest, and _____

fields _____ where _____ they lay _____ keep - ing their
to _____ the _____ earth it _____ gave _____ great
there _____ it _____ did both _____ stop _____ and

sheep, on a cold win - ter's night _____ that
light, and _____ so it con - tin - ued both
stay, right _____ o - ver the place _____ where

was _____ so deep. } No - el, No -
day _____ and night. }
Je - sus lay. }

el, No - el, No - el, born is the

King _____ of Is - ra - el.

1.2.3. 2. They _____ el.
3. This _____

4.

4. Then entered in those Wise Men three,
   Full rev'rently upon their knee,
   And offered there in His presence,
   Their gold and myrrh and frankincense.
   Noel, Noel, Noel, Noel,
   Born is the King of Israel.

31

FOR UNTO US A CHILD IS BORN
(From Handel's "Messiah")

By G.F. HANDEL

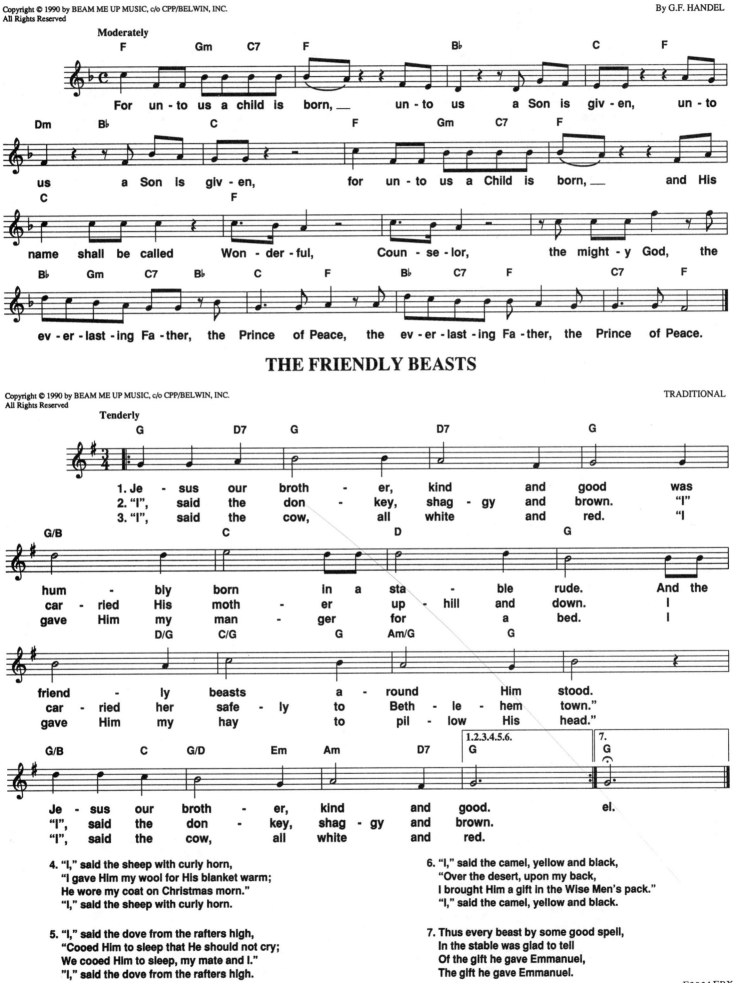

THE FRIENDLY BEASTS

TRADITIONAL

4. "I," said the sheep with curly horn,
"I gave Him my wool for His blanket warm;
He wore my coat on Christmas morn."
"I," said the sheep with curly horn.

5. "I," said the dove from the rafters high,
"Cooed Him to sleep that He should not cry;
We cooed Him to sleep, my mate and I."
"I," said the dove from the rafters high.

6. "I," said the camel, yellow and black,
"Over the desert, upon my back,
I brought Him a gift in the Wise Men's pack."
"I," said the camel, yellow and black.

7. Thus every beast by some good spell,
In the stable was glad to tell
Of the gift he gave Emmanuel,
The gift he gave Emmanuel.

F3021FBX

FROM HEAVEN ABOVE TO THE EARTH I COME

FROM OUR HOUSE TO YOURS

Words and Music by
LISA ANGELLE and
JOHN ACHWEERS

'cause you mean so much. From our house to yours, may eve-ry-one be blessed. May this Christ-mas be ___ the best, from our house to yours. 2. Old mem-o- And may this Christ-mas be ___ the best, from our house to yours. *(Spoken:) Merry Christmas!*

2. Old memories and mistletoe,
Cards signed with love hang in a row;
That feeling of Christmas fills the air.
The manger scene, the star above
Remind us all God sends His love.
May His spirit follow you throughout the year.

FUM, FUM, FUM

TRADITIONAL

On this joy-ful Christ-mas day sing Fum, Fum, Fum. On this joy-ful Christ-mas day sing
Thanks to God for hol-i-days sing Fum, Fum, Fum. Thanks to God for hol-i-days, sing

Fum, Fum, Fum. ___ For a bless-ed Babe was born up-on this day at break of morn. ___ In a
Fum, Fum, Fum. ___ Now we all our voi-ces raise, and sing a song of grate-ful praise, ___ Cel-e-

man-ger poor and low-ly lay the Son of God most ho-ly, Fum, Fum, Fum.
brate in song and sto-ry, all the won-ders of his glo-ry, Fum, Fum, Fum.

GESÙ BAMBINO
(The Infant Jesus)

Words by FREDERICK H. MARTENS
Music by PIETRO A. YON

GLAD CHRISTMAS BELLS

TRADITIONAL

1. Glad __ Christ-mas bells your __ mu-sic tells the __ sweet and pleas-ant sto-ry, how He came to earth in __ low-ly birth, the __ Lord of life and glo-ry.

2. No palace hall its ceiling tall
His kingly head spread over,
There only stood a stable rude
The heavenly Babe to cover.

3. Nor raiment gay as there He lay,
Adorn'd the infant stranger;
Poor humble child of mother's mild,
She laid Him in a manger.

4. But from afar, a splendid star
The wise men westward turning;
The livelong night saw pure and bright,
Above His birthplace burning.

GO TELL IT ON THE MOUNTAIN

TRADITIONAL

1. When I was a sin-ner, I prayed both night and day; I asked the Lord to aid me, and He showed me the way;
2. When I was a seek-er, I sought both night and day; I asked the Lord to help me, and He taught me how to pray.
3. Down in a low-ly man-ger the hum-ble Christ was born; God sent out sal-va-tion that bless-ed Christ-mas morn.

Go tell it on the moun-tain, o-ver the hills and ev-ery-where; go tell it on the moun-tain, that Je-sus Christ __ is born. born.

F3021FBX

GOD REST YE MERRY, GENTLEMEN

TRADITIONAL

Verses:
1. God rest ye merry, gentlemen; let nothing you dismay. Remember, Christ our Savior was born on Christmas Day to save us all from Satan's pow'r when we were gone astray. O tidings of comfort and joy, comfort and joy! O tidings of comfort and joy.
2. (In) Bethlehem, in Israel, this blessed Babe was born, and laid within a manger upon this blessed morn; the which His Mother Mary did nothing take in scorn.
3. (From) God our heav'nly Father, a blessed angel came; and unto certain shepherds brought tidings of the same; how that in Bethlehem was born the Son of God by name.
4. (The) shepherds at those tidings rejoiced much in mind; and left their flocks a-feeding, in tempest, storm and wind; and went to Bethlehem straightway, the Son of God to find.

GOOD CHRISTIAN MEN, REJOICE

Words by JOHN MASON NEALE
Music TRADITIONAL

Good Christian men, rejoice with heart and soul and voice.
Give ye heed to what we say: News! News! Jesus Christ is born today
Now ye hear of endless bliss: Joy! Joy! Jesus Christ was born for this.
Now ye need not fear the grave: Peace! Peace! Jesus Christ was born to save.
Ox and ass before Him bow, and He is in the manger now.
He hath ope'd the heav'nly door, and man is blessed evermore.
Calls you one and calls you all to gain His everlasting hall.
Christ is born today! Christ is born today! Good
Christ was born for this; Christ was born for this. Good
Christ was born to save; Christ was born to save.

GOOD KING WENCESLAS

Words by JOHN MASON NEALE
Music TRADITIONAL

Moderately

1. Good King Wen-ces-las looked out on the feast of
2. "Hith-er, page, and stand by me, it thou know'st it,
3. "Bring me flesh and bring me wine, bring me pine logs

Ste-phen, when the snow lay 'round a-bout, deep and crisp and
tell-ing, yon-der peas-ant, who is he? Where and what his
hith-er. Thou and I will see him dine, when we bear him

e-ven. Bright-ly shone the moon that night, though the frost was
dwell-ing?" "Sire, he lives a good league hence, un-der-neath the
thith-er." Page and mon-arch forth they went, forth they went to-

cru-el, when a poor man came in sight, gath-'ring win-ter,
moun-tain; right a-gainst the for-est fence, by Saint Ag-nes
geth-er, through the rude wind's wild la-ment and the bit-ter

1.2. fu-el. found-tain." weath-er.
3.

4. "Sire, the night is
5. In his mas-ter's

dark-er now, and the wind blows strong-er. Fails my heart, I
steps he trod, where the snow lay dint-ed. Heat was in the

know not how, I can go no long-er." "Mark my foot-steps,
ver-y sod which the Saint had print-ed. There-fore, Chris-tian

my good page, tread thou in them bold-ly. Thou shalt find the
men, be sure, wealth or rank pos-sess-ing; ye who now will

1. G
2. G

win-ter's rage freeze thy blood less cold-ly."
bless the poor shall your-selves fing bless-ing.

F3021FBX

GRANDMA GOT RUN OVER BY A REINDEER!

Words and Music by
RANDY BROOKS

2. Now we're all so proud of Grandpa,
   He's been taking this so well.
   See him in there watching football,
   Drinking beer, and playing cards with Cousin Mel.
   It's not Christmas without Grandma.
   All the family's dressed in black,
   And we just can't help but wonder:
   Should we open up her gifts or send them back?
   (To Chorus:)

3. Now the goose is on the table,
   And the pudding made of fig,
   And the blue and silver candles,
   That would just have matched the hair in Grandma's wig.
   I've warned all my friends and neighbors,
   Better watch out for yourselves.
   They should never give a license
   To a man who drives a sleigh and plays with elves.
   (To Chorus:)

HALLELUJAH CHORUS

(From Handel's "Messiah")

By G.F. HANDEL

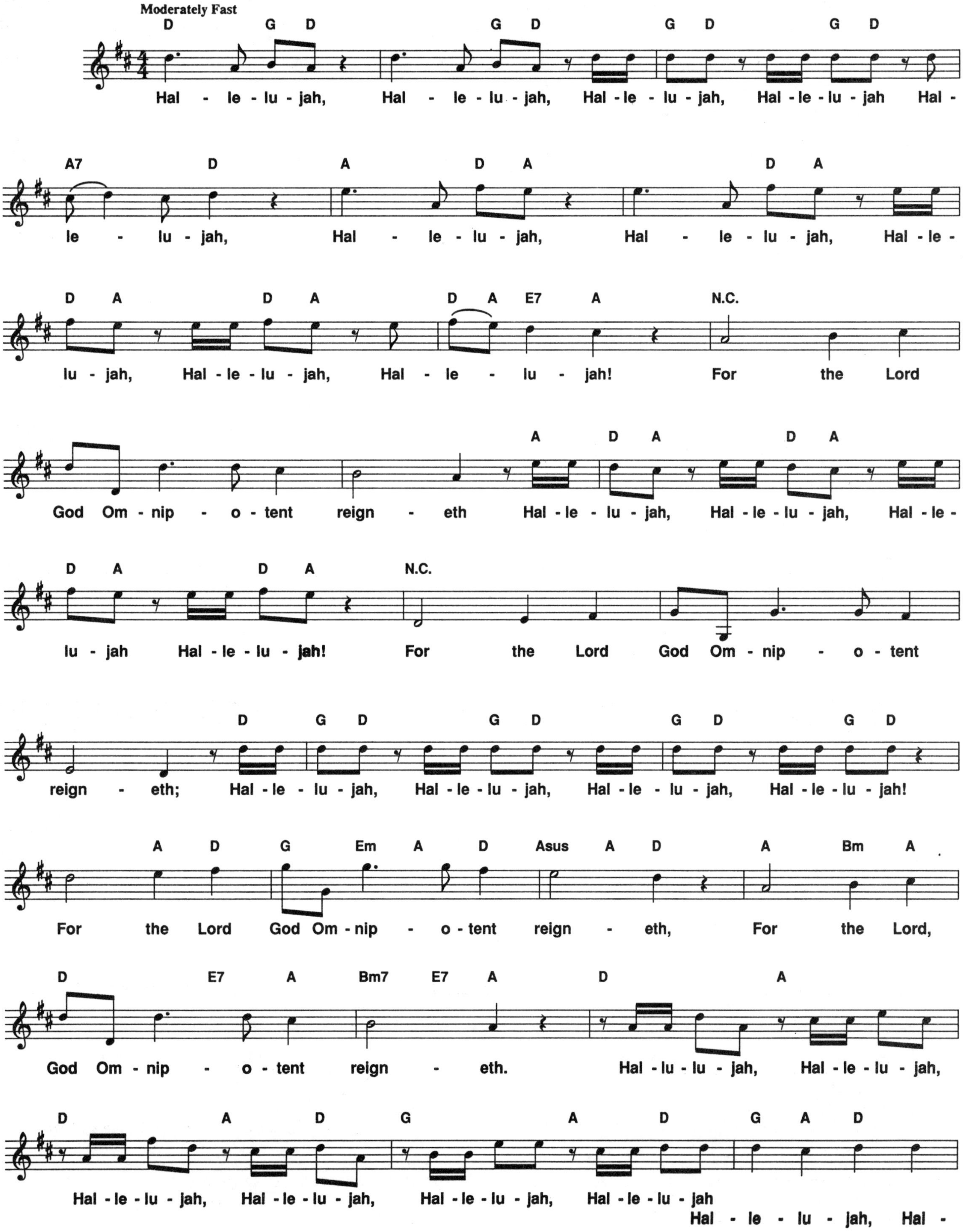

F3021FBX

42

HARK! THE BELLS ARE RINGING

TRADITIONAL

Brightly

| G | | Gdim | G | | A7 | D7 | G |

Hark the bells are ring-ing gay, 'tis the eve of Christ-mas Day. Hol-i-days have

| Gdim | G | | D7 | G | D | D7 | G |

now be-gun, full of mer-ri-ment and fun. Mer-ri-ly we pass our time.

| D | D7 | G | | Gdim | G | D7 | G |

Mer-ry as the Christ-mas time. May the com-ing New Year too, Be a hap-py one to you.

HARK! THE HERALD ANGELS SING

Words by CHARLES WESLEY
Music by FELIX MENDELSSOHN

Moderately

| G | | D | G/B | G | G/D | D | G/B | Bm | C | G/D | D | G |

1. Hark! The her-ald an-gels sing, ___ "Glo-ry to the new-born King!
2. Christ by high-est heav'n a-dored; ___ Christ the ev-er-last-ing Lord!
3. Hail the heav'n born Prince of Peace! ___ Hail the Son of Right-eous-ness!

| D | Em | G/D | A7/C# | | Bm | A7/C# | D | Gmaj7 | A7 | D |

Peace on earth and mer-cy mild, ___ God and sin-ners re-con-ciled."
Late in time be-hold Him come, ___ off-spring of a Vir-gin's womb.
Light and life to all He brings, ___ ris'n with heal-ing in His wings.

| N.C. | | G/D | D7/F# | G | G/D | D | N.C. | | G/B | D7/F# | G | G/D | D |

Joy-ful all ye na-tions rise; ___ join the tri-umph of the skies; ___
Veiled in flesh the God-head see; ___ hail the in-car-nate De-i-ty. ___
Mild He lays His glo-ry by, ___ born that man no more may die. ___

| C | | E7 | Am | E7 | Am | D7/C | G/B | | G/D | D | G |

with an-gel-ic host pro-claim, "Christ is ___ born in Beth-le-hem!"
Pleased as man with man to dwell, Je-sus, ___ our Em-man-u-el!
Born to raise the sons of earth; born to ___ give them sec-ond birth.

| C | | E7 | Am | E7/G# | Am | D7/C | G/B | **1.2.** G/D | D | G | **3.** G/D | D | G |

Hark! The her-ald an-gels sing, "Glo-ry ___ to the new-born King!" new-born King!"

HAVE YOURSELF A MERRY LITTLE CHRISTMAS

Words and Music by
HUGH MARTIN
and RALPH BLANE

F3021FBX

HERE COMES SANTA CLAUS
(Right Down Santa Claus Lane)

Words and Music by
GENE AUTRY and
OAKLEY HALDEMAN

Here comes San-ta Claus, here comes San-ta Claus right down San-ta Claus lane.

Vix - en and Blitz - en and all his rein - deer are pull - ing on the reign.
He's got a bag that is filled with toys for the boys and girls a - gain.
He does - n't care if you're rich or poor, for he loves you just the same.
He'll come a - round when the chimes ring out, then it's Christ - mas morn a - gain

Bells are ring - ing, chil - dren sing - ing, all is mer - ry and bright.
Hear those sleigh - bells jin - gle, jin - gle; what a beau - ti - ful sight.
San - ta knows that we're God's chil - dren; that makes ev - ery - thing right.
Peace on earth will come to all if we just fol - low the light.

Hang your stock - ings and say your pray'rs,
Jump in bed, cov - er up your head,
Fill your hearts with a Christ - mas cheer
Let's give thanks to the Lord a - bove
'cause San - ta Claus comes to - night. night.

HERE WE COME A-CAROLING
(The Wassail Song)

TRADITIONAL

1. Here we come a car - ol - ing a - mong the leaves so green.
(2) are not dai - ly beg - gars that beg from door to door. But
(3) bless the mas - ter of this house, like - wise the mis - tress too. And

Here we come a wan - d'ring so fair to be seen.
we are neigh - bor's chil - dren whom you have seen be - fore.
all the lit - tle chil - dren that 'round the ta - ble go.
Love and joy come to

you, and to you glad Christ - mas too. And God bless you and send you a hap - py New

Year, and God send you a hap - py New Year. 2. We Year.
3. God

THE HOLLY AND THE IVY

TRADITIONAL

From the Videocraft T.V. Musical Spectacular "RUDOLPH THE RED-NOSED REINDEER"

A HOLLY JOLLY CHRISTMAS

By JOHNNY MARKS

F3021FBX

(There's No Place Like)
HOME FOR THE HOLIDAYS

Words by AL STILLMAN
Music by ROBERT ALLEN

HOW GREAT OUR JOY!

German Melody Arranged by
HUGO JUNGST

Brightly

1. While by my sheep we watched at night. Glad tid - ings
2. There shall be born, so he did say, in Beth - le -
3. There shall the child lie in a stall; this child who
4. This gift of God we'll cher - ish well; that ev - er

brought an an - gel bright
hem a Child to - day.
shall re - deem us all.
joy our hearts shall fill.

} How great our joy! (Great our

joy!) Joy, joy, joy! (Joy, joy, joy!)

Praise we the Lord in heav'n on high. Praise we the

Lord in heav'n on high.

1.2.3. heav'n on high.

4. heav'n on high.

I AM SO GLAD ON CHRISTMAS EVE

PEDER KNIDSON
Translated by Bernard Gasso

Moderately

1. I am so glad _____ on Christ - mas Eve, the
2. I am so glad _____ on Christ - mas Eve, my

night of Je - sus' birth: _____ that's when a star _____ shone
praise - es rise _____ a - bove _____ to Je - sus Who _____ has

like the sun and an - gles sang _____ on earth. _____
brought to earth the Par - a - dise _____ of love. _____

F3021FBX

I BELIEVE IN SANTA CLAUS

Words and Music by
DOLLY PARTON

I SAW THREE SHIPS

TRADITIONAL

1. I saw three ships come sail - ing in on Christ - mas Day, on
2. what was in those ships all three on Christ - mas Day, on
3. Vir - gin Mary and Christ were there on Christ - mas Day, on

Christ - mas Day. I saw three ships come sail - ing in on
Christ - mas Day. And what was in those ships all three on
Christ - mas Day. The Vir - gin Mary and Christ were there on

Christ - mas Day in the morn - ing. 2. And
Christ - mas Day in the morn - ing? 3. The
Christ - mas Day in the morn - ing.

I WANT AN OLD-FASHIONED CHRISTMAS

Words by FLORENCE TARR
Music by FAY FOSTER

I want an old - fash - ioned Christ - mas, with toys and gifts for all, with

stock - ings hang - ing from the fire - place, and a pine - tree stand - ing tall. I

want an old - fash - ioned Christ - mas to feel the soft cold __ snow, and

home - folks cheer - i - ly nod - ding a mer - ry warm __ "Hel - lo!"

I want to hear the lit - tle

chil - dren __ sing - ing the Christ - mas __ car - ols I used to know; and

hear the ev-'ning church bells ring-ing out their joy-ous wel-come of long a-
go. I want an old-fash-ioned Christ-mas, to
be a child a-gain, to make be-lieve that there's a San-ta,
for I was hap-pi-est then. Mer-ry Christ-mas! Mer-ry Christ-mas!
Mer-ry Christ-mas!

I WONDER AS I WANDER

Words and Music by
JOHN JACOB NILES

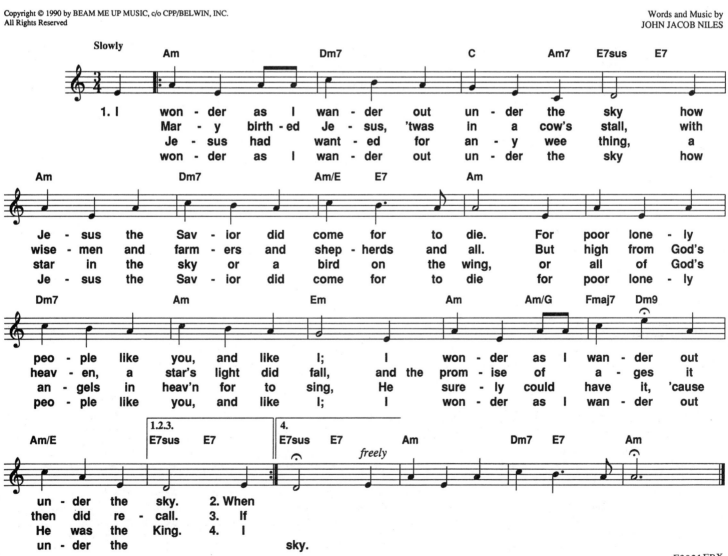

1. I won-der as I wan-der out un-der the sky how
Mar-y birth-ed Je-sus, 'twas in a cow's stall, with
Je-sus had want-ed for an-y wee thing, a
won-der as I wan-der out un-der the sky how

Je-sus the Sav-ior did come for to die. For poor lone-ly
wise-men and farm-ers and shep-herds and all. But high from God's
star in the sky or a bird on the wing, or all of God's
Je-sus the Sav-ior did come for to die for poor lone-ly

peo-ple like you, and like I; I won-der as I wan-der out
heav-en, a star's light did fall, and the prom-ise of a-ges it
an-gels in heav'n for to sing, He sure-ly could have it, 'cause
peo-ple like you, and like I; I won-der as I wan-der out

un-der the sky. 2. When
then did re-call. 3. If
He was the King. 4. I
un-der the sky.

F3021FBX

I HEARD THE BELLS ON CHRISTMAS DAY
(Popular)

Words by HENRY WADSWORTH LONGFELLOW
Adapted by JOHNNY MARKS
Music by JOHNNY MARKS

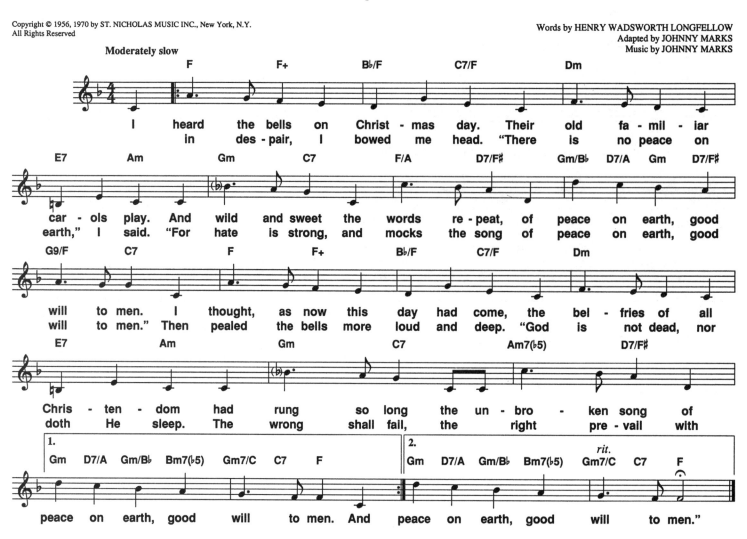

I heard the bells on Christ - mas day. Their old fa - mil - iar
in des - pair, I bowed me head. "There is no peace on

car - ols play. And wild and sweet the words re - peat, of peace on earth, good
earth," I said. "For hate is strong, and mocks the song of peace on earth, good

will to men. I thought, as now this day had come, the bel - fries of all
will to men." Then pealed the bells more loud and deep. "God is not dead, nor

Chris - ten - dom had rung so long the un - bro - ken song of
doth He sleep. The wrong shall fail, the right pre - vail of with

peace on earth, good will to men. And peace on earth, good will to men."

I HEARD THE BELLS ON CHRISTMAS DAY
(Traditional)

Words by HENRY WADSWORTH LONGFELLOW
Music by HENRY BISHOP

1. I heard the bells on Christ - mas day. Their old fa - mil - iar
   thought how, as the day had come, the bel - fries of all

car - ols play. And wild and sweet the words re - peat of
Christ - en - dom had rolled a - long the un - bro - ken song of

peace on earth, good will to men. 2. I
peace on earth, good will to men. 3. And will to men.

3. And in despair I bowed my head:
   "There is no peace on earth." I said,
   "For hate is strong and mocks the song
   Of peace on earth, good will to men."

4. Then pealed the bells more loud and deep:
   "God is not dead, nor doth He sleep;
   The wrong shall fail, the right prevail,
   With peace on earth, good will to men."

5. Till, ringing, singing on its way,
   The world revolv'd from night to day.
   A voice, a chime, a chant sublime,
   Of peace on earth, good will to men!

I'LL BE HOME FOR CHRISTMAS

Lyric by KIM GANNON
Music by WALTER KENT

F3021FBX

INFANT HOLY, INFANT LOWLY

Paraphrase by EDITH M.G. REED
W. ZLOBIE LEZY (POLISH CAROL)

IT CAME UPON THE MIDNIGHT CLEAR

Words by EDMUND HAMILTON SEARS
Music by RICHARD STORRS WILLIS

IT'S THE MOST WONDERFUL TIME OF THE YEAR

By EDDIE POLA
and GEORGE WYLE

Bright waltz tempo

It's the most won-der-ful time _____ of the year, _____
hap - hap-pi-est sea - son of all _____

with the kids jin-gle bell-ing, and ev-'ry-one tell-ing you, "Be of good
with those hol-i-day greet-ings, and gay hap-py meet-ings when friends come to

cheer." _____ It's the most won-der-ful time _____ of the
call. _____ It's the hap - hap-pi-est sea - son of

year. _____ It's the all. _____

There'll be part-ies for host-ing, marsh-mal-lows for toast-ing and car-ol-ing

out in the snow. There'll be scar-y ghost sto-ries and tales of the

glo-ries of Christ-mas-es long, long a-go. _____ It's the most

won-der-ful time _____ of the year. _____ There'll be much mis-tle-

toe-ing and hearts will be glow-ing, when loved ones are near. _____ It's the

most won-der-ful time of the year. _____

F3021FBX

JESU, JOY OF MAN'S DESIRING

By J.S. BACH

F3021FBX

From the Videocraft T.V. Musical Spectacular "RUDOLPH THE RED-NOSED REINDEER"

JINGLE, JINGLE, JINGLE

By JOHNNY MARKS

JINGLE BELLS

Words and Music by
JAMES PIERPONT

JOLLY OLD ST. NICHOLAS

TRADITIONAL

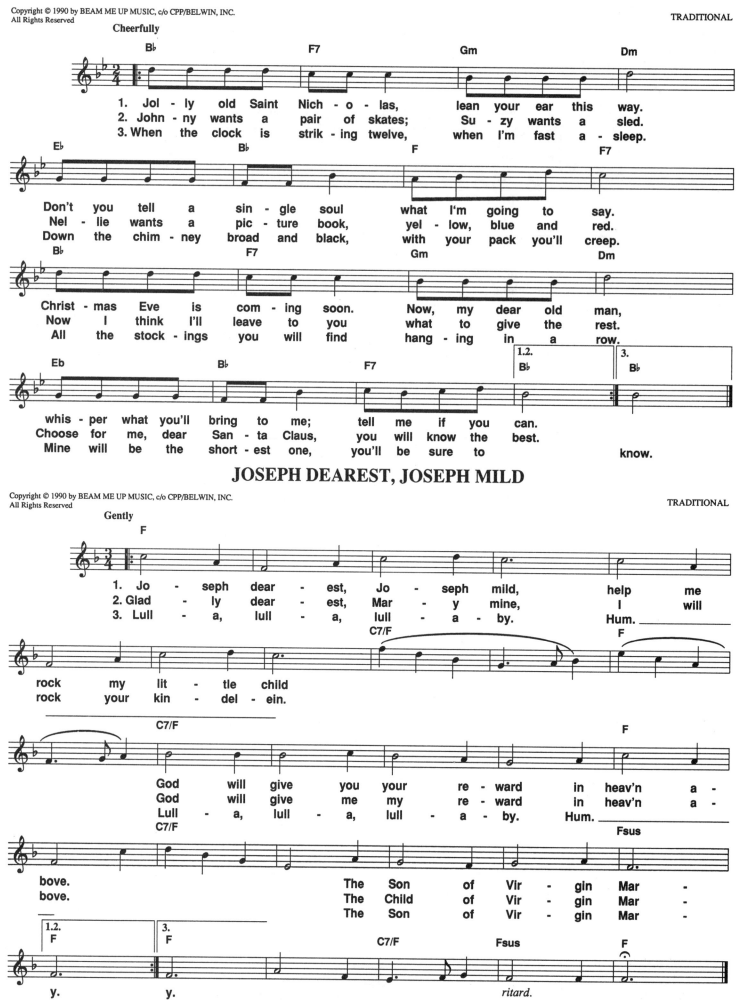

Cheerfully

1. Jol - ly old Saint Nich - o - las, lean your ear this way.
2. John - ny wants a pair of skates; Su - zy wants a sled.
3. When the clock is strik - ing twelve, when I'm fast a - sleep.

Don't you tell a sin - gle soul what I'm going to say.
Nel - lie wants a pic - ture book, yel - low, blue and red.
Down the chim - ney broad and black, with your pack you'll creep.

Christ - mas Eve is com - ing soon. Now, my dear old man,
Now I think I'll leave to you what to give the rest.
All the stock - ings you will find hang - ing in a row.

whis - per what you'll bring to me; tell me if you can.
Choose for me, dear San - ta Claus, you will know the best.
Mine will be the short - est one, you'll be sure to know.

JOSEPH DEAREST, JOSEPH MILD

TRADITIONAL

Gently

1. Jo - seph dear - est, Jo - seph mild, help me
2. Glad - ly dear - est, Mar - y mine, I will
3. Lull - a, lull - a, lull - a - by. Hum.

rock my lit - tle child
rock your kin - del - ein.

God will give you your re - ward in heav'n a -
God will give me my re - ward in heav'n a -
Lull - a, lull - a, lull - a - by. Hum.

bove. The Son of Vir - gin Mar -
bove. The Child of Vir - gin Mar -
The Son of Vir - gin Mar -

y.
y.
y.

ritard.

JOY TO THE WORLD

Words by ISAAC WATTS
Music by LOWELL MASON

JOYOUS CHRISTMAS

Words and Music by
JOHNNY MARKS

F3021FBX

LET ALL MORTAL FLESH KEEP SILENCE

Liturgy of St. James Translated
by GERARD MOULTRIE
PICARDY (FRENCH CAROL)

LET IT SNOW! LET IT SNOW! LET IT SNOW!

Lyric by SAMMY CAHN
Music by JULE STYNE

LET US GO, O SHEPHERDS

TRADITIONAL COLOMBIAN CAROL
Translated by BERNARD GASSO

THE LITTLE DRUMMER BOY

Words and Music by
KATHERINE DAVIS, HENRY ONORATI
and HARRY SIMEONE

LITTLE SAINT NICK

Words and Music by
BRIAN WILSON

2. Just a little bobsled, we call it Old Saint Nick,
   But she'll walk the toboggan with a four-speed stick.
   She's a candyapple red with a ski for a wheel.
   And when Santa gives the gas, man, just watch her peel.
   (To Chorus:)

3. He's haulin' through the snow at a fright'nin' speed
   With a half dozen deer with a Rudy to lead.
   He's got to wear goggles, 'cause the snow really flies,
   And he's cruisin' every pad with a little surprise.
   (To Chorus:)

LO, HOW A ROSE E'ER BLOOMING

TRADITIONAL

1. Lo, how a rose e'er bloom - ing from ten - der
2. I - sa - iah 'twas fore - told it, from the rose I

stem hath sprung. Of Jes - se's lin - eage com - ing as men of
have in mind. With Mar - y we be - hold it, as the vir - gin

old have sung. It came a flow'r - et bright, a - mid the
moth - er kind. To show God's love a - right she bore to

cold of win - ter, when half spent was the night, was the night.
men a sav - ior, when half spent

LOOK AROUND YOU, IT'S CHRISTMAS TIME

By BOBBY GOLDSBORO

1. San - ta Claus on ev - 'ry cor - ner as he braves the win - ter night.

Bells are ring - in' in his left hand and a bot - tle in his right.

Look a - round you, it's Christ - mas time.

2. Christmas trees made out of plastic
Standing bare in every door.
We will deck the halls with holly
If we make it off the floor.
Look around you, it's Christmas time.

3. Father's celebrating Christmas
With a bottle full of rum,
While his children wait for presents
That they know will never come.
Look around you, it's Christmas time.

4. We can't buy Christmas presents
And we have none yet to send,
Wait until we get our presents
So we'll know how much to spend.
Look around you, it's Christmas time.

5. A one arm beggar selling pencils,
But we cannot spare a dime,
Save it for the parking meter
We may have to pay a fine.
Look around you, it's Christmas time.

6. All the churches filled with nothing
But the quiet of the night.
Doesn't anyone remember
Why we celebrate tonight?
Look around you, it's Christmas time.

THE MAN WITH ALL THE TOYS

Words and Music by
BRIAN WILSON

2. How thrilled that someone must have been,
And he must have been tempted to go in.
He stayed out in the cold, and
When he left them, he told about
The man with all the toys.

MARCH OF THE TOYS

Music by
VICTOR HERBERT

MERRY CHRISTMAS

Lyrics by JANICE TORRE
Music by FRED SPIELMAN

MASTERS IN THIS HALL

TRADITIONAL

Brightly
Verse:

1. Mas - ters in this hall, _____ hear ye news to - day _____
2. Then to Beth - le'm town, _____ we went two in two. _____
3. Ox and ass Him know _____ kneel - ing on their knee.
4. This is Christ, the Lord. _____ Mas - ters, be ye glad.

brought from o - ver - seas, and ev - er you I pray.
And in sor - ry place _____ heard the ox - en low.
Won - drous joy had I this lit - tle Babe to see.
Christ - mas is come in, and no folk should be sad.

Chorus:

1.2.3. Now - ell! Now - ell! Now - ell! Now - ell, sing we
4. Now - ell! Now - ell! Now - ell! Now - ell, sing we

clear! Holp - en are all folk on earth. _____ Born _____
loud! God to - day hath poor fold rais - ed, and _____

1.2.3.
is God's son so dear.

4.
cast a - down the proud.

(Joyeux Noel, Buon Natale, Feliz Navidad)

A MERRY, MERRY CHRISTMAS TO YOU

By JOHNNY MARKS

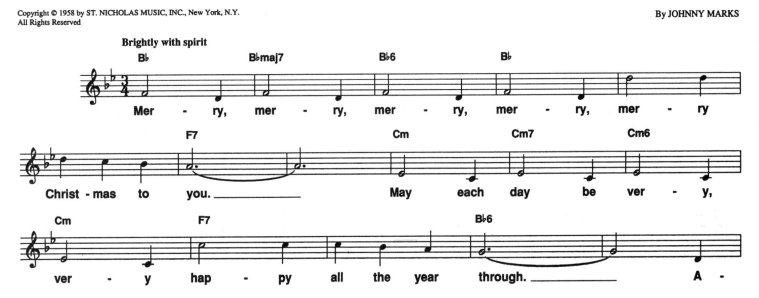

Brightly with spirit

Mer - ry, mer - ry, mer - ry, mer - ry, mer - ry

Christ - mas to you. _____ May each day be ver - y,

ver - y hap - py all the year through. _____ A -

MY CHRISTMAS COLORING BOOK

Words and Music by
WARNER WILDER

Verse 2:
Color Him Prince of Peace; this miracle man,
Doing His mighty works all over the land.
He brought the greatest gift the world could think of.
Color Him beautiful; He gave you His love.

Verse 3:
Color His robe with white, this prophet of good,
Showing the only way to one brotherhood.
Bring Him the greatest gift that you could think of.
Color Him beautiful, color Him love.

MERRY CHRISTMAS, MY DARLING

Words and Music by
DALE EVANS

From The Videocraft T.V. Musical Spectacular "RUDOLPH THE RED-NOSED REINDEER"

THE MOST WONDERFUL DAY OF THE YEAR

By JOHNNY MARKS

NESTOR, THE LONG-EARED CHRISTMAS DONKEY

Words and Music by
GENE AUTRY, DON PFRIMMER
and DAVE BURGESS

* optional recitation provided at the bottom of this page should be used before the song begins.

1. Nes-tor was a don-key who sel-dom laughed or played, 'cause no one ev-er used him in the sta-ble where he stayed. All the cam-els teased him and the oth-er don-keys too. They said, "Look at lit-tle Nes-tor, there's ___ noth-ing he ___ can do."

Chorus:

Look at lit-tle Nes-tor, he's got ears that drag ___ the ground. They whis-pered as they mocked him, but he heard ev-'ry sound. Nes-tor's heart was bro-ken and his eyes were full of tears. If on-ly there was some-thing he could do a-bout ___ his ears.

Recitation (ad lib.)
Ev'ryone knows about Rudolph, our fleetfooted friend from the north
Who lights Santa's way thru the darkness as he drives his sleigh back and forth.
But there's someone else we should mention if we want the whole story told;
He carried the first gift of Christmas, more precious than diamonds or gold.

2. One dark night two strangers gave Nestor a surprise;
   They chose him from all others, for they loved his gentle eyes.
   The man was called by Joseph, and Mary was his bride.
   She needed help to Bethlehem and Nestor's back to ride.

3. They traveled through the desert, but hadn't gone too far,
   When winter clouds no longer let them see their guiding star.
   But Nestor has a secret, only he could hear the sound,
   As the Angels gave directions to the ears that dragged the ground.
   (Chorus:)

4. And so it was that Nestor found the manger where they stayed,
   Where kings and wisemen bowed before a baby where he laid.
   Mary bore our Savior and Nestor brought them there,
   A gift of love from God above for all the world to share.

5. Though Rudolph I just love you, I know you'd want it said,
   Nestor's ears are lovely as a reindeer's nose is red.
   So, children, if you're happy when you trim your Christmas trees,
   You might thank a little donkey whose ears hang to his knees.

Last Chorus:
   Look at little Nestor, he's got ears that drag the ground,
   They shouted as they praised him,
   And his friends all gathered 'round.
   Nestor's heart grew happy and his eyes held no more tears,
   Now all the world knows Nestor, for his laughter and his ears.

F3021FBX

THE NUTCRACKER SUITE
OVERTURE

Music by
PETER ILYICH TCHAIKOVSKY

(The Nutcracker Suite)

MARCH

Music by
PETER ILYICH TCHAIKOVSKY

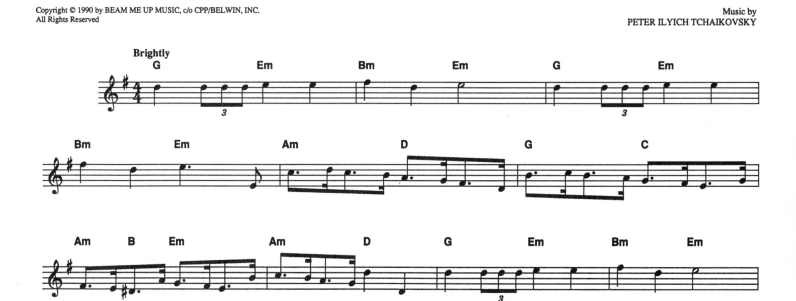

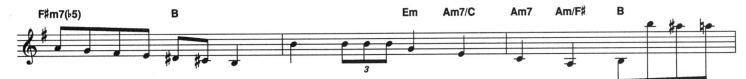

(The Nutcracker Suite)

DANCE OF THE SUGAR-PLUM FAIRY

Music by
PETER ILYICH TCHAIKOVSKY

(The Nutcracker Suite)

RUSSIAN DANCE (Trepak)

Music by
PETER ILYICH TCHAIKOVSKY

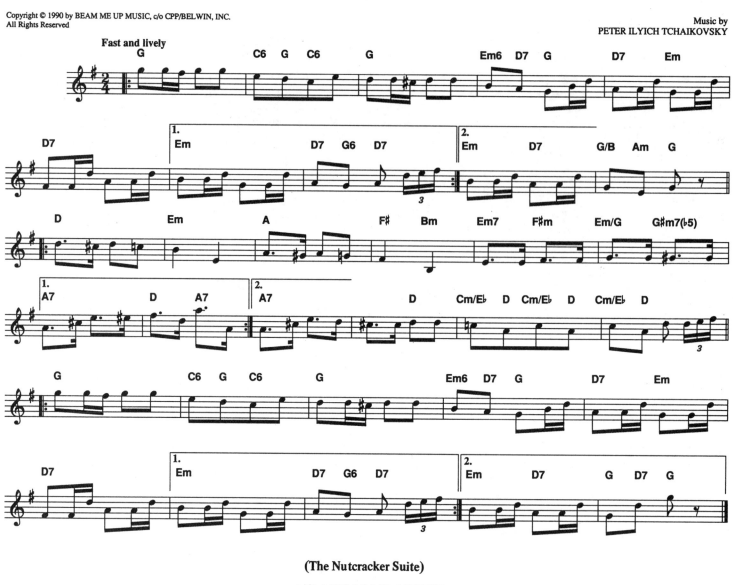

(The Nutcracker Suite)

ARABIAN DANCE

Music by
PETER ILYICH TCHAIKOVSKY

(The Nutcracker Suite)

CHINESE DANCE

Music by
PETER ILYICH TCHAIKOVSKY

(The Nutcracker Suite)

DANCE OF THE REED FLUTES

Music by
PETER ILYICH TCHAIKOVSKY

F3021FBX

(The Nutcracker Suite)

WALTZ OF THE FLOWERS

Music by
PETER ILYICH TCHAIKOVSKY

THE NIGHT BEFORE CHRISTMAS SONG

Music by JOHNNY MARKS
Lyrics adapted by JOHNNY MARKS
from Clement Moore's Poem

'Twas The Night Be-fore Christ-mas and all thru the house, not a crea-ture was stir-ring not e-ven a
up to the house-top the rein-deer soon flew, with a sleigh full of toys and St. Nich-o-las

mouse. All the stock-ings were hung by the chim-ney with care, in the hope that St. Nich-o-las
too. Down the chim-ney he came with a leap and a bound. He was dressed all in fur and his

soon would be there. Then what to my won-der-ing eyes should ap-pear, a min-ia-ture
bel-ly was round. He spoke not a word but went straight to his work And filled all the

sleigh and eight ti-ny rein-deer. A lit-tle old driv-er so live-ly and quick, I
stock-ings; then turned with a jerk. And lay-ing his fin-ger a-side of his nose, then

knew in a mo-ment it must be St. Nick. And more rap-id than ea-gles his rein-deer all
giv-ing a nod up the chim-ney he rose. But I heard him ex-claim as he drove out of

came, as he shout-ed, "On Dash-er" and each rein-deer's name. *(Spoken) Look - Here comes*
sight, "Mer-ry Christ-mas to all and to *opt. Rudolph!*

And so all a Good Night!"

NOEL! NOEL!

TRADITIONAL

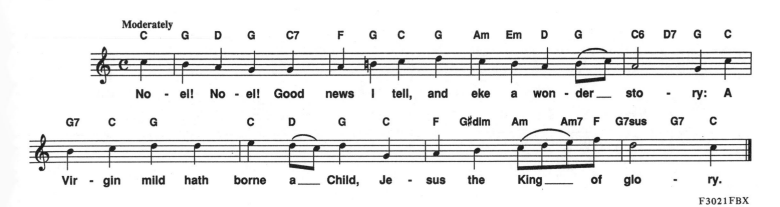

No-el! No-el! Good news I tell, and eke a won-der sto-ry: A

Vir-gin mild hath borne a Child, Je-sus the King of glo-ry.

F3021FBX

82

O CHRISTMAS TREE
(O Tannenbaum)

Moderately

1. O Christ-mas tree, O Christ-mas tree, thy leaves are so un-chang-ing. O
(2. O) Christ-mas tree, O Christ-mas tree, you fill all hearts with gai-ety. O
(3. O) *Tan-nen-baum, O Tan-nen-baum, wie treu sind die-ne Blät-ter. O*

Christ-mas tree, O Christ-mas tree, thy leaves are so un-chang-ing. Not
Christ-mas tree, O Christ-mas tree, you fill all hearts with gai-ety. On
Tan-nen-baum, O Tan-nen-baum, wie treu sind die-ne Blät-ter. Du

on-ly green when sum-mer's here, but al-so when 'tis cold and drear. O
Christ-mas Day you stand so tall, af-ford-ing joy to one and all. O
grünst nicht nur zur Som-mer-zeit, nein auch im Win-ter wenn es schneit. O

Christ-mas tree, O Christ-mas tree, thy leaves are so un-chang-ing. 2. O Blät-ter.
Christ-mas tree, O Christ-mas tree, you fill all hearts with gai-ety. (3. O)
Tan-nen-baum, O Tan-nen-baum, wie treu sind dei-ne

O COME, ALL YE FAITHFUL
(Adeste Fideles)

English Words by FREDERICK OAKELEY
Latin Words Attributed to JOHN FRANCIS WADE
Music by JOHN READING

Broadly

1. O come, all ye faith-ful, joy-ful and tri-um-phant, O
(2. O) sing, choirs of an-gels, sing in ex-ul-ta-tion; O
3. Yea, Lord we greet Thee born this hap-py morn-ing;

come ye, O come ye to Beth-le-hem.
sing all ye cit-i-zens of heav'n a-bove.
Je-sus, to Thee be glo-ry giv'n.

Come and be-hold Him, born the King of an-gels.
Glo-ry to God in the high-est. } O
Word of the Fa-ther, now in flesh ap-pear-ing.

come, let us a-dore Him; O come let us a-dore Him, O

come let us a-dore Him, Christ, the Lord. 2. O Lord.

O COME, LITTLE CHILDREN

Words and Music by
CHRISTOPH VON SCHMIDT
and J. A. P. SCHULZ

1. O come lit-tle chil-dren, from cot and from hall. O
(2.) hay is His pil-low, the man-ger His bed. The
(3.) "Glo-ry to God" sing the an-gels on high. "And

come to the man-ger in Beth-le-hem's stall. There meek-ly He
beasts stand in won-der to gaze on His head. Yet there where He
peace up-on earth" heav'n-ly voic-es re-ply. Then come lit-tle

li-eth, the heav-en-ly Child, so poor and so
li-eths so weak and so poor, come shep-herds and
chil-dren, and join in the lay that glad-dened the

hum-ble, so sweet and so mild. 2. The Day
wise men to kneel at His door. 3. Now
world on that first Christ-mas

O COME, O COME EMMANUEL

TRADITIONAL

1. O come, o come, Em-man-u-el, and
(2) come, thou Day-spring, come and cheer our
(3) come, thou wis-dom from on high, and
(4) come, de-sire of na-tions bind in

ran-som cap-tive Is-ra-el. That mourns in lone-ly
spir-its by thine ad-vent here. Dis-perse the gloom-y
or-der all things far and nigh. To us the path of
one the hearts of all man-kind. Bid thou our sad di-

ex-ile here, un-til the Son of God ap-pear.
clouds of night, and death's dark shad-ows put to flight.
know-ledge show, and cause us in her ways to go.
vi-sions cease, and be Thy-self our King of peace. } Re-

joice, re-joice! Em-man-u-el shall

come to thee, O Is-ra-el. 2. O el.
3. O
4. O

F3021FBX

O HOLY NIGHT

Words by JOHN SULLIVAN DWIGHT
Music by ADOLPHE CHARLES ADAM

O LITTLE TOWN OF BETHLEHEM

Words by PHILLIPS BROOKS
Music by LEWIS H. REDNER

Moderately

1. O lit - tle town of Beth - le - hem, how still we ___ see thee
(2.) Christ is born of Mar - y, and gath - ered ___ all a -
(3.) si - lent - ly, how si - lent - ly the won - d'rous ___ gift is
(4.) ho - ly Child of Beth - le - hem, de - scend to ___ us we

lie. A - bove thy deep and dream - less sleep the
bove while mor - tals sleep, and an - gels keep their
giv'n. So God im - parts to hu - man hearts the
pray. Cast out our sin and en - ter in. Be

si - lent ___ stars go by. Yet in thy dark streets shin - eth the
watch of ___ won - d'ring love. O morn - ing stars to - geth - er pro -
bless - ings ___ of His heav'n. No ear may hear His com - ing. But
born in ___ us to - day. We hear the Christ - mas an - gels. The

ev - er last - ing light. The hopes and fears of
claim the ho - ly birth. And prais - es sing to
in the world of sin where meek souls will re -
great glad tid - ings tell: O come to us, a -

1.2.3. | 4.
all the years are met in thee to - night. 2. For el.
God the King, and peace to men on earth. 3. How
ceive Him still, the dear Christ en - ters in. 4. O
bide with us, our Lord Em - man - u -

O SANCTISSIMA

TRADITIONAL

Joyfully

O thou hap - py. ___ O thou ho - ly. ___
Day of ho - li - ness, ___ Peace and hap - pi - ness, ___

glo - rious peace bring - ing Christ - mas time.
joy - ful, glo - ri - ous Christ - mas Day.

An - gel throngs to meet Thee; on Thy birth we greet Thee;
An - gels tell the sto - ry of this day of glo - ry;

all ___ hail ___ Je - sus, our Sav - ior King.
praise ___ Christ, our Sav - ior, born this Christ - mas Day.

O WORSHIP THE KING

TRADITIONAL

O wor-ship the King all glo-rious a-bove, O grate-ful-ly sing His pow'r __ and His love. Our Shield and De-fen-der, the An-cient of days, Pa-vil-ioned in splen-dor and gird-ed with praise.

ODE TO JOY

by LUDWIG VAN BEETHOVEN

AN OLD-FASHIONED CHRISTMAS

Words and Music by
JOHNNY MARKS

There's noth-ing like An Old-Fash-ioned Christ-mas ___ With hol-ly on the door; ___ And a bright Christ-mas tree for the whole fam-i-ly, With pre-sents all o-ver the floor. ___ There's noth-ing like the old fav-'rite car-ols ___ When neigh-bors come to call ___ So the best I can wish you, ___ is An Old Fash-ioned Christ-mas, that's all. ___

ONCE IN ROYAL DAVID'S CITY

Words by MRS. C.F. ALEXANDER
Music by H.J. GAUNTLETT

1. Once in roy-al Da-vid's cit-y stood a low-ly cat-tle shed, where a moth-er laid her Ba-by in a man-ger for His bed. Mar-y was that moth-er mild, Je-sus Christ her lit-tle Child. He is gone.
2. He came down to earth from heav-en, who is God and Lord of all, and His shel-ter was a sta-ble, and His cra-dle was a stall. With the poor and mean and low-ly lived on earth our Sav-ior ho-ly
3. And our eyes at last shall see Him through His own re-deem-ing love; for that Child so dear and gen-tle is our Lord in heav-en a-bove. And He leads His chil-dren on to the place where

F3021FBX

OVER THE RIVER AND THROUGH THE WOODS

TRADITIONAL

PATAPAN

TRADITIONAL

RING OUT, WILD BELLS

Words by ALFRED, LORD TENNYSON
Music by WOLFGANG AMADEUS MOZART

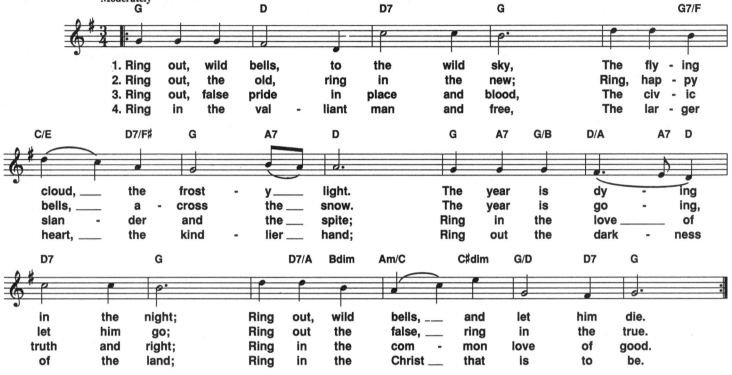

1. Ring out, wild bells, to the wild sky, The fly-ing
2. Ring out, the old, ring in the new; Ring, hap-py
3. Ring out, false pride in place and blood, The civ-ic
4. Ring in the val-liant man and free, The lar-ger

cloud, the frost-y light. The year is dy-ing
bells, a-cross the snow. The year is go-ing,
slan-der and the spite; Ring in the love of
heart, the kind-lier hand; Ring out the dark-ness

in the night; Ring out, wild bells, and let him die.
let him go; Ring out the false, ring in the true.
truth and right; Ring in the com-mon love of good.
of the land; Ring in the Christ that is to be.

RISE UP, SHEPHERD, AND FOLLOW

TRADITIONAL

1. There's a star in the East on Christ-mas morn.
(2) take good heed to the an-gels's words.
Rise up shep-herd and

fol-low. It will lead to the place where the sav-ior's born.
You'll for-get your flocks, you'll for-get your herds.

Rise up shep-herd and fol-low. Fol-low, fol-low;

rise up shep-herd and fol-low. Fol-low the star of

Beth-le-hem. Rise up shep-herd and fol-low. 2. If you fol-low.

F3021FBX

ROCKIN' AROUND THE CHRISTMAS TREE

By JOHNNY MARKS

From the Videocraft Musical Spectacular "RUDOLPH THE RED-NOSED REINDEER"

RUDOLPH, THE RED-NOSED REINDEER

Words and Music by
JOHNNY MARKS

F3021FBX

SANTA CLAUS IS COMIN' TO TOWN

Words by HAVEN GILLESPIE
Music by J. FRED COOTS

THE SANTA CLAUS PARADE

Words and Music by
JOHNNY MARKS

THE SECRET OF CHRISTMAS

Words by SAMMY CAHN
Music by JAMES VAN HEUSEN

SILENT NIGHT

Words and Music by
JOSEPH MOHR and
FRANZ GRUBER

(There's Nothing Like)
AN OLD FASHIONED CHRISTMAS

Words and Music by
JOHNNY MARKS

96

THE SIMPLE BIRTH

TRADITIONAL

SING WE NOEL

FRENCH CAROL

2. Angels adore and praise in glorious strain;
Mortals repeat the glad refrain!
Bright in the East a fair and shining star
Guided the wise men from afar.
Let all the earth rejoice and sing
And heav'n with hallelujahs ring!
Sing we Noel, Noel, Noel.

3. O'er all the earth our glad hosannas ring;
Hail we the Christ, the new-born King.
Shout the glad tidings of the Saviour's birth,
Good will to men and peace on earth.
Now is He come, your homage bring,
All hail the new-born infant King!
Sing we Noel, Noel, Noel.

SING WITH JOY

TRADITIONAL

1. Sing with joy, 'tis Christ - mas morn. Un - to us a Child is born; Christ has come on earth to dwell. God with us; Im - man - u - el.
2. Shep - herds watch - ing through the night, won - d'ring at the daz - zling light; Christ has come on an - gel tell of the hope of Is - ra - el.
3. Thou - sand, thou - sand an - gels raise songs of glad tri - um - phant praise; sing - ing through the star - ry sky, glo - ry be to God on high!

SLEEP, O SLEEP, MY LOVELY CHILD

TRADITIONAL ITALIAN

Sleep o sleep, my love - ly Child. King di - vine. Peace be Thine. Slum - ber gent - ly, slum - ber sweet - ly, King di - vine. Peace be Thine. Sleep, o sleep, o King, o Dear One. Fa la la la, fa la la la la, fa la la la, fa la la la la. Fa la la la la la, fa la la la la la la, fa la la la.

SLEIGH RIDE

Lyric by MITCHELL PARISH
Music by LEROY ANDERSON

STAR OF THE EAST

Words bt GEORGE COOPER
Music by AMANDA KENNEDY

SING, O SING, THIS BLESSED MORN

TRADITIONAL GERMAN

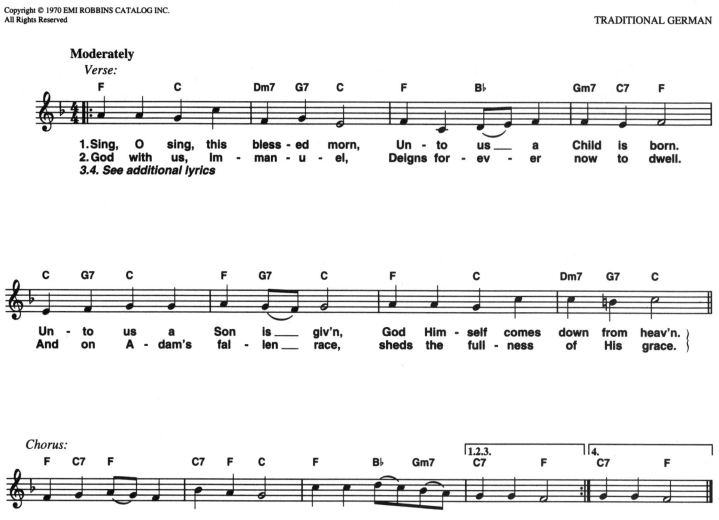

Verse 3:
God comes down that man may rise
Lifted by Him to the skies;
Christ is Son of man that we
Sons of God in Him may be.
(To Chorus:)

Verse 4:
O renew us, Lord we pray,
With Thy spirit day by day;
That we ever one may be
With the Father and with Thee.
(To Chorus:)

THERE IS NO CHRISTMAS LIKE A HOME CHRISTMAS

Words by CARL SIGMAN
Music by MICKEY J. ADDY

F3021FBX

THIRTY-TWO FEET AND EIGHT LITTLE TAILS
(Dasher, Dancer, Prancer, Vixen, Comet, Cupid, Donner, Blitzen)

by JOHN REDMOND, JAMES CAVANAUGH
and FRANK WELDON

From "BABES IN TOYLAND"

TOYLAND

Lyric by GLEN MACDONOUGH
Music by VICTOR HERBERT

'TWAS IN THE MOON OF WINTER TIME
(THE HURON CHRISTMAS CAROL)

English words by J.E. MIDDLETON
Original Huron words by FATHER JEAN DE BREBEUF
Music TRADITIONAL

THE TWELVE DAYS OF CHRISTMAS

TRADITIONAL

THE UKRANIAN CAROL

Music by M. LEONTOVICH

UP ON THE HOUSETOP

Words and Music by
BENJAMIN RUSSELL HANBY

A VIRGIN UNSPOTTED

TRADITIONAL

2. Then God sent an angel from Heaven so high,
To certain poor shepherds in fields where they lie,
And bade them no longer in sorrow to stay,
Because that our Savior was born on this day.
(Refrain)

3. Then presently after, the shepherds did spy
Vast numbers of angels to stand in the sky;
They joyfully talked and sweetly did sing:
"To God be all glory, our heavenly King."
(Refrain)

4. To teach us humility all this was done,
And learn we from thence haughty pride for to shun:
A manger His cradle who came from above,
The great God of mercy, of peace and of love.
(Refrain)

THE VIRGIN'S SLUMBER SONG

English Words by EDWARD TESCHEMACHER
Music by MAX REGER

F3021FBX

From the Videocraft Musical Spectacular "RUDOLPH THE RED-NOSED REINDEER"

WE ARE SANTA'S ELVES

By JOHNNY MARKS

Ho! Ho! Ho! Ho! Ho! Ho! We are San - ta's elves! We are San - ta's elves fill - ing San - ta's shelves with a toy for each girl and boy. Oh, we are San - ta's elves! We work hard all day, but our work is play. Dolls we try out, see if they cry out. We are San - ta's elves! We've a spe - cial job each year, we don't like to brag. Christ - mas Eve we al - ways fill San - ta's bag! _____ San - ta knows who's good, do the things you should! And we bet you, he won't for - get you. We are San - ta's elves! elves! Ho! Ho! Ho! Ho! Ho! Ho! We are San - ta's elves, Ho! Ho!

WE THREE KINGS OF ORIENT ARE

Words and Music by
JOHN HENRY HOPKINS

Moderately

1. We three kings of O - ri - ent are, bear - ing gifts we tra - verse a - far, field and foun - tain, moor and moun - tain, fol - low - ing yon - der star.
2. Born a King on Beth - le - hem's plain, gold I bring to crown Him a - gain, King for - ev - er, ceas - ing nev - er, o - ver us all to reign.
3. Frank - in - cense to of - fer have I, in - cense owns a De - i - ty nigh. Pray'r and prais - ing all men rais - ing, wor - ship Him, God most high.
4. Myrrh is mine, its bit - ter per - fume, breathes of life of gath - er - ing gloom; sor - row - ing, sigh - ing, bleed - ing, dy - ing, sealed in the stone - cold tomb.
5. Glo - rious now be - hold Him a - rise, King and God and Sac - ri - fice. Al - le - lu - ia, al - le - lu - ia, Earth _____ to heav'n re - plies.

O, _____ star of won - der, star of night, star with roy - al beau - ty bright; west - ward lead - ing still pro - ceed - ing, guide us to Thy per - fect light. light.

F3021FBX

110

WE WISH YOU A MERRY CHRISTMAS

TRADITIONAL

WELCOME CHRISTMAS

Lyrics by DR. SEUSS
Music by ALBERT HAGUE

WHAT CHILD IS THIS?

Words by WILLIAM CHATTERTON DIX
Music TRADITIONAL

WHEN CHRISTMAS MORN IS DAWNING

TRADITIONAL

2. When Christmas morn is dawning,
He comes from Heav'n above,
To take away the sins of man,
With words and thoughts of love,
To take away the sins of man,
With words and thoughts of love.

3. When Christmas morn is dawning,
Oh, Jesus, do come in,
And may I never cause Thee grief,
Or pain with mortal sin,
And may I never cause Thee grief,
Or pain with mortal sin.

F3021FBX

WHEN SANTA CLAUS GETS YOUR LETTER

Music and Lyrics by
JOHNNY MARKS

WHILE SHEPHERDS WATCHED THEIR FLOCKS BY NIGHT

Words by NAHUM TATE and NICHOLAS BRODY
Music by GEORGE FREDERICK HANDEL

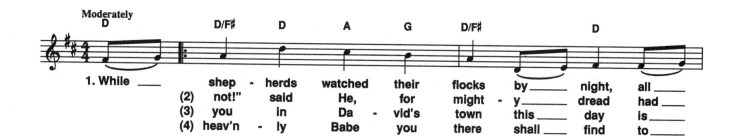

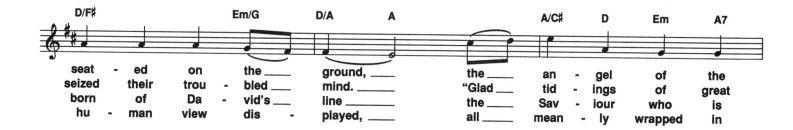

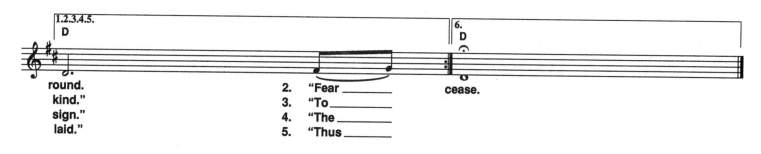

5. Thus spoke the Seraph and forthwith
   Appeared a shining throng
   Of angels praising God, who thus
   Addressed their joyful song,
   Addressed their joyful song.

6. All glory be to God on high,
   And to the earth be peace,
   Good will hence forth from heav'n to men,
   Begin and never cease,
   Begin and never cease.

WITH BELLS ON

Words and Music by
DOLLY PARTON

A Cat In The Hat Presentation from MGM - Television Dr. Seuss' "HOW THE GRINCH STOLE CHRISTMAS"

YOU'RE A MEAN ONE MR. GRINCH

Lyrics by DR. SEUSS
Music by ALBERT HAGUE

1. You're a mean one Mis - ter Grinch; you really are a heel. You're as cud - dly as a cac - tus, you're as charm - ing as an eel. Mis - ter Grinch! You're a bad ba - nan - a with a greas - y black peel.

2. You're a with Ar - sen - ic sauce!

2. You're a monster Mr. Grinch!
   Your heart's an empty hole.
   Your brain is full of spiders,
   You've got garlic in your soul!
   Mr. Grinch!
   I wouldn't touch you with a
   Thirty-nine and
   One half-foot pole.

3. You're a foul one Mr. Grinch!
   You're a nasty-wasty skunk!
   Your heart is full of unwashed socks,
   Your soul is full of gunk,
   Mr. Grinch!
   The three words that best describe you
   Are as follows and I quote:
   Stink! - Stank! - Stunk!

4. You're a vile one Mr. Grinch!
   You have termites in your smile.
   You have all the tender sweetness
   Of a seasick crocodile,
   Mr. Grinch! - - - - - -
   (spoken) And given the choice between
   The two of you
   I'd take the seasick crocodile.

5. You're a rotter Mr. Grinch!
   You're the king of sinful sots.
   Your heart's a dead tomato
   Splotched with moldy, purple spots.
   Mr. Grinch - - - - -
   (spoken) Your soul is an appalling
   Dumpheap overflowing with the most
   Disgraceful assortment of deplorable
   Rubbish imaginable, mangled up in
   - - Tangled up knots.

6. You nauseate me Mr. Grinch!
   With a nauseous, super naus.
   You're a crooked jerkey jockey
   And you drive a crooked hoss,
   Mr. Grinch! - - - - -
   (spoken) You're a three-decker Sauerkraut
   And toadstool sandwich
   - - With arsenic sauce.

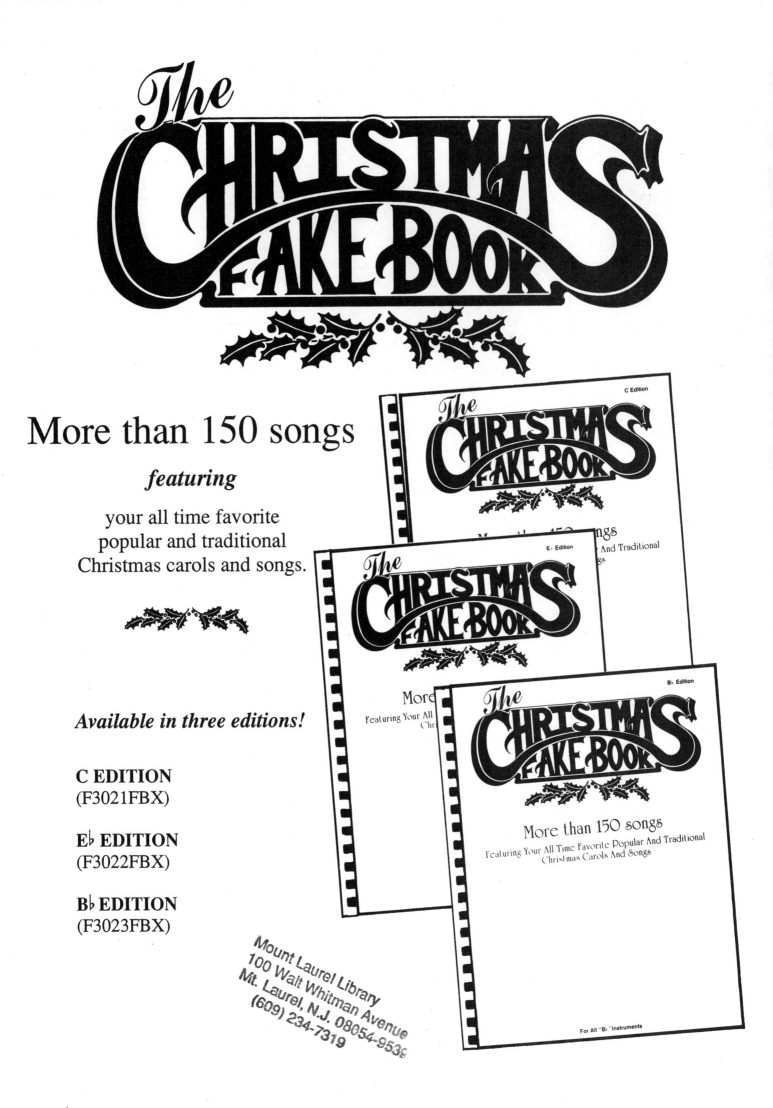